How to Be Your Own General Contractor

Everything You Need to Know to Take Control and Save Thousands on Your Renovation or New Construction

PETER GLAW

Published by Premier Press
PremierPress.ca

Cover and Interior Design by Lauretta Stevens

Disclaimer

For further information, contact:
Peter Glaw
info@premier-renovations.com
www.premier-renovations.com
1-905-286-0303

Table of Contents

Foreword

Premier's Access Card saved us $150K on our $820K renovation project!

In mid-2017, my wife and I were looking to renovate our house. Like most people, our two biggest concerns were quality and price, but we also only wanted to do this once, so we were looking for higher-end finishes and materials that would last (and that we would be happy with) for decades. So we interviewed several contractors and eventually settled on one with excellent references and a great track record. The next step of the process involved design and practical considerations, and it quickly became apparent that the costs would be problematic – we were exceeding our budget with even the very basic materials, floorplans, etc. Not willing to compromise on quality or the reputation of the contractor, at that point we had essentially resolved to put off the renovation and continue trying to save.

It was then that we met Peter Glaw of Premier Quality Renovations Inc., and he introduced us to the idea of being our own contractors. Given that I'm self-employed, and my wife works part-time, even though it would mean more time and attention on our part, it seemed like an ideal option. Premier provided access to their suppliers, the tradespeople he relies on for his own jobs, and also provided guidance, support, and advice through each stage. We ended up completing our reno in December 2018, and for the price of 3 floors of a basic renovation with our original contract, we were able to renovate the 3 floors, AND the basement, AND with the highest end appliances, flooring, lighting, etc.

Now, there are several key things worth mentioning when it comes to being your own contractor because it's important to not sugarcoat it. First of all, it is very time-consuming – some days you will not need to be on your job site at all, while at other times you'll be there most of the day. Regardless, you will be on the phone or emailing a lot and your mind and focus will be on your project at all times. It will also be stressful; there will be confusion and delays and mistakes, and it can be very frustrating. And it will be expensive; renos are expensive, regardless of whether you are your own contractor or you're using someone else. Those are the main harsh realities of the process, but they're inevitable, I think, for every job.

For the positives, you will know your house better than you ever did before. You will know what went into building each element, and you will get to know reliable, honest people who can service or repair everything if ever anything happens. You will also get to choose anything and everything in your house – every knob and hinge and piece of wood etc., and the house will be done exactly how you want it. And most importantly, being your own contractor, you will save a lot of money – In our experience, I would say between 15%-20% and maybe more which, given today's reno prices, could represent hundreds of thousands of dollars. The process is not easy, but it's doable. I don't have any experience in renovations or building – I'm not even very handy – but with Premier's help, a little research, and a willingness to learn, we came away with a beautiful full-house gut reno.

And a word about Peter Glaw and Premier Quality Renovations Inc. – Peter and his team are available in a way that very few people are … Day or night, rain or shine, inside or outside the country, Peter and his team are a phone call away. He has answers for every question, and people for every job. His experience makes him familiar with each and every element of building a house, with a group of tradespeople who have been whittled down and selected based on years of him working with them, being 100% sure of the quality of their work and their reliability. Peter and his team are enthusiastic about building, and vehement about his high standards for good, solid, enduring work. He will care about your project, and that's reflected in the people who work for him, and it's also reflected in how much he oversees you and your job. He will make sure you're on schedule, make sure you're not being taken advantage of, and make sure the job is being done properly. Being your own contractor is tough, but it's rewarding in many ways, and if you're up to the task, there's very few people better suited to help you through it.

Pat and Danielle, Toronto

Before
Premier Renovations

After
Premier Renovations

Dedication

This book is dedicated to the people who have had a big part in influencing my life and success.

To my parents Gerhard & Irmgard. My father taught me everything about the discipline required to take pride in every job I do. My mother's unconditional love and support have always been my rock.

My two wonderful sons Brandon & Tristan. You are my entire World. Being your father is my life's greatest gift, and I'm so very proud of the men you've become. Tristan for the incredibly hard work you do on the intense development of our systems and website.

Carl & Terry at Hyperweb Communications for our website creation, development and content.

Michelle, Office and Social Media Manager, for her ongoing support and valued dedication.

David Shiang, Lauretta Stevens and Rick McCulloch without each of you this book wouldn't exist. You took our work ethics along with our vision and assembled it here to educate plus help homeowners in becoming their own General Contractor.

And finally, the homeowners themselves. You are the reason I get out of bed every morning.

Being a part of creating your dream space is the drive and thrust in my life.

I thank you all immensely.

Peter Glaw

Dedication

Introduction

Each year across North America, homeowners spend hundreds of billions of dollars renovating their homes and building new ones. A significant and growing fraction of these projects are managed by the homeowners themselves rather than by general contractors. There are any number of reasons why homeowners decide to tackle the job themselves, ranging from the desire to save money to the wish to control the process. When you are the boss, you are ultimately responsible for the outcome of the project.

Before you decide to tackle a job that may cost hundreds of thousands of dollars and involving dozens of third parties over many months, it is a good idea to know what you are facing. You need to determine whether you have the necessary skills and desire. There is no mystery to doing the work of a general contractor, but it is not for the faint of heart. Having been in the renovation and remodeling business for my entire life, I can assure you that anyone can do it … as long as they are good learners, can get along with people, well organized, and have a good attitude. Of course, there are other factors such as finances, negotiation skills, and the ability to respond when things don't always go according to plan. But you don't have to know how to pour cement, hang a shingle, or even use a hammer. You will be managing other people, much like an orchestra leader conducts the virtuosos who play the instruments.

RenoMark
Certificate of Completion
is hereby granted to

Peter Glaw
Premier Quality Renovations Inc.

to certify that they completed to satisfaction
The Professional Renovator Education Program
Granted: July 22, 2020

Dave Wilkes, President & CEO, BILD   Jack H. Torossian, Chair, Renovator Executive Committee

The News Mississauga
Proudly presents

Premier Quality Renovations
winner of the Silver

READERS' CHOICE
AWARD

SILVER WINNER 2013
The Mississauga News

in the category of

Best Home Improvements

Who Am I and Why I Wrote This Book

For as long as I can remember, I've been involved in the construction industry. I may not have been playing with an erector set at age 1, but I do remember hanging around my Dad and his shop from an early age. He was a builder and a cabinet maker, and I was surrounded by all things carpentry. Building and creating dream spaces became part of my DNA.

While my friends were clocking in their hours at the local eateries and retail stores as part of their summer jobs, I spent my high school summers helping my father out building houses and doing renovation projects. That paved the way towards starting my own company.

Peter Glaw

I continued with my passion, first buying homes, renovating them and selling them. Because my foundation in the industry came from building and construction, craftsmanship and attention to detail were second nature. Word of mouth about my work spread quickly, and I've been able to build a company that fits my family's lifestyle.

We've opened up a Premier Renovations Consulting Division where my team and I consult with homeowners around the world on their projects. You can be your own GC and rely on our proven Premier System for unbiased, professional advice no matter where you are located. I can help from the design phase of your project all the way through to the final touches. I evaluate designs, bids, materials, timetables, construction, workmanship, etc. I make sure that you are getting a fair deal and that you are not being taken advantage of.

With smartphones and laptops now in widespread use, you can take me anywhere inside or outside your home, letting me peer over your shoulder just as if I were standing beside you. It doesn't matter whether you are in the Greater Toronto Area or on the other side of the planet. Quality standards vary around the world and also depend on how much you are paying. What may be a great bargain in one location could be highway robbery in another. My job is to make sure you are getting what you pay for, if not a bit more.

In addition, the need for enhanced safety and security is more important than ever. With more people working from home and spending more of their leisure time at home, they are increasingly renovating and upgrading. Why hire someone who is going to be in and out of your house for what could be months on end when you can do it yourself with a little bit of remote help? See the section at the end of the book about my company for more information.

We've also launched our Exclusive Premier Access Card program across North America. This card is a must have for all homeowners embarking on an improvement project or renovation. In the Greater Toronto Area, we've identified hundreds of suppliers and tradespeople who will give you up to 60% off retail prices. So, while your neighbour may pay $100,000 for a job, you may be able to get it done for $70,000 or even less. You'll never pay full retail again. And Toronto is just the start. We're rolling out the program across major cities in North America. People everywhere love saving money.

At the end of the book, I'll give you more details.

Having been in the industry for over 41 years and worked on thousands of projects ranging from small jobs to building new homes, I've seen my share of the good, the bad, and the ugly. My industry has more than its fair share of horror stories, and I recently read that we're considered just a step up from used car salespeople. Even though the vast majority of general contractors are competent and hardworking people, I've seen too many rip-offs, too much bad workmanship, and too many disappointed homeowners. A lot of them have asked for my advice on how to get the job done, and in addition to being a builder, I consult with people all over the continent (and increasingly from other parts of the world) who want to manage their own projects.

Being a general contractor isn't rocket science, but no one has explained the job the way I see it and also provided on-demand consulting services to anyone in the world who wants help. That's why I wrote this book. It will give you all the basics you need to take control of your own project and see it to a successful completion. After reading my book, you may decide that you'd be better off hiring someone, and that's okay. At least you'll be much more knowledgeable than the typical homeowner. I've seen far too many people overpay for their jobs and get less quality than they should.

Projects by Premier Quality Renovations.

See www.premier-renovations.com for hundreds more.

So You're Thinking About Being Your Own General Contractor

You've decided it's the right time to renovate your home or build a new one. With all the choices available when it comes to getting the job done, it can be a daunting task to figure out where you should start. If someone you know can refer you to a competent professional, that might be all you need. You can go online and register with any number of services that will bring professionals who advertise on the platform to your inbox. You can also seek out firms you may have heard about through local advertising or word of mouth.

Most people start by engaging the services of professionals such as contractors, architects, and interior designers. And then there are plumbers, carpenters, electricians, and building inspectors who will also be involved in helping you create your masterpiece. You want to start off on the right foot so that your project goes smoothly, and nothing gets overlooked.

If you are reading this book, you are thinking of being your own General Contractor. However, you will likely also need the services of an architect or interior designer. (If you can be your own GC and do the design work of an architect and interior designer, my hat is off to you.) Either of them should be able to help you with the design part of the project if they have the right level of experience. Why call one vs another? What are the specialties of each? What are the questions you need to ask to make sure you choose wisely?

There are numerous pitfalls that lie in wait, even for the experienced homeowner, and my job is to help you avoid them. The tips outlined here will prepare you for a successful process. I want you to get the best bang for your buck … while avoiding the horror stories that are all-too common in the industry.

Let's look at the two major professions involved in the design phase of a project before moving onto General Contractors.

Architects

Architects are licensed professionals like contractors, but they must also have an advanced degree to become a professional architect. Usually, architects have a Masters in Architecture, which takes about two years to complete on top of a Bachelor's degree. Architects will listen to your hopes and dreams for the remodeling project, look at any drawings or pictures you like, discuss your budget, then draw up a plan to bring it to reality. An architect's involvement could end there, or you could hire them to manage the entire project, much like you would with a contractor. In such a case, the architect would select a preferred contractor suitable to work with.

Architects have an "outside in" or "big picture" view of the world. They are often called upon to design entire buildings or even complexes such as shopping centres or neighbourhoods. Because of the scope of their work and the fact that they have advanced degrees that require the passing of rigorous exams, they tend to think of themselves at the top of the totem pole. They have a command of building technologies, structural safety, the environment, and regulations, more than most contractors or designers, but many don't understand kitchen spacing, industry guidelines, or the aesthetics of interior design.

Architects often charge by the hour, or if they are overseeing the entire project, they will charge a project fee. Some architects won't get involved in a project unless the budget is $100K or higher; others have more flexibility.

Interior Designers

Interior Designers have an "inside out" view of the world in that they start by imagining the possibilities in the space you are trying to create and then figuring out how to fill it. They know space planning, colour coordination, lighting, cabinetry, fixtures, tiling, and paint. They may call in an architect, but it depends on the work you want done. If your job is a simple renovation, with new cabinets and fixtures replacing old ones, there may be no need for any structural work like tearing down walls. But if you are looking at a renovation requiring any kind of expansion or new construction, you may need an architect.

Like architects and contractors, interior designers use their expertise to create appealing ideas for making your dreams a reality, given your budget and time frame. A basic design might include the floor plan, cabinets, appliances, and a new paint job. A full-service design might include a new layout, new materials, and trips to exclusive showrooms where you can see the latest innovations.

Anyone can say that they are a designer, and you don't have to have a degree or certification in order to do design work. However, there are organizations that certify kitchen and bath designers so that the public can distinguish between those who have rigorous training vs. those who don't. The National Kitchen and Bath Association (NKBA) is North America's leading trade association for the kitchen and bath industry. It provides tools, research, certification, and events to thousands of professionals. To become certified requires several years of training that covers everything from space planning to colour to lighting to fixtures to construction.

Interior Designers typically charge $100 to $240 per hour – a fee similar to what an architect would charge – although architects tend to charge more than designers. Some designers set a minimum project fee of, say, $5,000, unless they are called in for a short consultation. Like architects and contractors, designers who manage the entire project will look at their out-of-pocket costs and then decide what they need to add to cover their overhead and have something left over. One design firm recommends thinking of 8 percent to 12 percent of your entire project as related to interior design, but this is just a rule of thumb.

General Contractors

You see their trucks everywhere you go. Contractors, General Contractors, Builders, Constructors, Construction Managers. Generally speaking, they are builders more than anything else. They supervise the entire project and give directions (under your ultimate supervision, of course) to all the subcontractors who perform the work so that everything goes according to plan. They are like an orchestra leader. If they are experienced, they may do some of the work themselves such as carpentry or painting. But they aren't structural engineers or architects or designers – they are builders. If specialists are required, it's their job to make sure that they are called in. Or you may have your favorite pro in mind, and you can ask your contractor to work with them.

Since this book is all about having you assume the role of a General Contractor (GC), let's get down to brass tacks and be clear on what is involved. What exactly does a GC do on a construction project?

While no two jobs are exactly alike, the GC is responsible for getting the job you want done. You hire them to manage the actual building or construction of your dream space. They take specifications from architects or designers and hire the right specialists to perform the necessary work. These specialists, called Subcontractors or Tradespeople, are carpenters, roofers, plumbers, electricians, masons, tile specialists, landscapers, etc. Even though they are independent contractors in their own right, they "work for" the GC on specific jobs. A good GC will have several jobs going at the same time requiring the use of different kinds of subcontractors for each job.

The GC makes sure that the necessary building supplies and fixtures are on hand when needed and schedules everybody so that the work to be done is performed in the right order and to the right specification.

Your relationship is first and foremost with the GC (who may or may not have anything to do with the design). Even though the subcontractors are doing the actual work, if something isn't right, you tell the GC, and they will (or are supposed to) take care of the problem.

Notes

Notes

Skills Needed to Be a Great General Contractor

When you become your own GC, you remove a level of management. Now all the subcontractors work directly for you. If things aren't going right, you need to take control and not rely on someone else.

What does it take to be a good GC? Here are a few of the required skills:

Planning

Negotiating

Scheduling and time management

Overseeing the big picture

Managing people and money

Delegating

Procuring materials and supplies

Hiring

Resolving problems

Dealing with inspectors and the permitting process

GC's must also know building codes, regulations, insurance, etc. Depending on their level of experience, they will know the latest in building technology (green buildings, smart homes, energy savings, communications, safety, etc.) If you are going to be your own GC, it would be hard for you to come up to speed on all of the latest technologies. During the onset of the 2020 pandemic, for example, a wide range of new building codes were implemented. We've been trained on the latest rules and regulations, and you can check out our website for our certifications. Rather than go through such training yourself, you'd be better off getting the guidance of an expert.

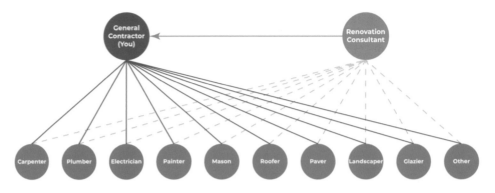

How much money does a GC make on a typical job? Are they worth it?

Generally speaking, the GC will add up the actual costs of a project (labour and supplies) and mark up the amount by a certain percent that may vary depending on the size and complexity of a project. For example, if the cost of subcontractors, materials, permits, etc. is $250,000, the GC may add on anywhere from 20%-50%. This will pay for the GC's time, expertise, overhead, and profit. In other words, you may be paying anywhere from $50,000 to $125,000 extra for the services of a GC, meaning that the cost of your project will be $300,000 to $375,000. These number of course will vary depending on several factors, and we will examine them later. And we're talking about a medium-size project.

Is the extra expense worth it? Only you can decide. Is your primary motivation to save money? If so, you may be able to have a $375,000 renovation for $250,000. That's a lot of savings. Or another way of looking at it is that your $375,000 buys you what someone else would pay up to $562,500 for. Think of all the extra touches your project will have if you GC it yourself. A better counter-top? A state-of-the-art security system? Upgraded appliances that will do everything but cook dinner for you? That's the case with a lot of homeowners we have helped.

Is your motivation to make sure you "have it your way," like the old Burger King ad promised? To be in control of your dream project? After all, no one is going to care more about your job than you. Many homeowners have found out far too late that someone cut corners and concealed problems that should have been identified during the course of the job. When you are in control, you call the shots. There is nobody to call other than the subcontractors you have hired.

Before you decide that you want to save tens or hundreds of thousands of dollars, you need to know what you are getting yourself into. What else do you need to be a successful GC? Besides the list above, you will need the money for the job (which can often be financed) and the following:

- Time
- Ability to do research (finding qualified help, bargains on supplies, etc.)
- Patience
- Adaptability
- Attention to Detail

Let's look at the biggest factors you should consider in more detail – Planning. Budgeting, Time, and Ability to Negotiate.

Planning

Before you even think about calling an architect, a landscaper, or a kitchen specialist, you need to know what kind of renovation or construction you want. If you plan far enough in advance, you can take advantage of seasonal sales on materials, closeouts, etc. And you may be able to get better rates from subcontractors if you schedule them farther out. Calling someone at the last minute often results in poor workmanship, extra costs, or both. The importance of planning your job and having a big picture in mind before you begin the actual work cannot be emphasized too much.

Put together a "dream scrapbook" with photos, ideas, articles, samples, reviews, and assorted odds and ends that you can refer to as you build out your project in your imagination. You may want to divide your scrapbook into various sections such as Kitchen, Bath, Basement, Living Room, Family Room, Patio, etc. Consult the websites, videos, TV shows, and media appearances of people (including myself) such as Mike Holmes, Bob Vila, Lou Manfredini, and

Bryan Baeumler for ideas.

You may also want to know what kind of renovation will be a good financial investment in addition to improving the quality of your life. If you are thinking about moving somewhere down the road after you have finished renovating, how much you will recoup in resale value will be important. We can guide you so that your renovation gives you the best return for your dollar. Although new kitchens and baths are always welcome, design trends come and go. You don't want to be renovating in a style that is going out of favor. Open concepts are in fashion these days and designing for remote work looks like a long-term trend.

Budgeting

It's fine to have big dreams about the kind of remodeling or renovation you want to undertake, but you will eventually have to come down to earth and determine how you are going to pay for everything. Unless you have the cash set aside, you are going to have to come up with additional money. This can come in the form of assets that you convert to cash or a loan from a bank, mortgage company, or similar financial institution. If you've got lots of equity built up in your home, perhaps a Home Equity Line of Credit (HELOC) will do. After all, you normally don't have to pay interest on such credit until you use it, unlike a traditional loan.

Whatever your source of funds, make sure that you establish a budget before you make a single call to the tradespeople who will actually do the work. As your project progresses, you may find that you can do more than you thought – nicer fixtures, better appliances, more finished living space – but don't count on suddenly coming into new sources of money.

Time

If you are going to be your own GC, you will be trading your time in return for spending less. But you might also be taking on what could be a series of headaches that last for months on end. Make sure you have the available time and patience to do the necessary research; evaluate tradespeople and suppliers; check out the latest designs, appliances, and fixtures; complete the required paperwork; schedule the right people at the right time, etc.

Devise a project schedule, knowing full well that things don't always go according to plan. In some project management circles, people say, "Things take twice as long and cost twice as much as you think." While this may be overly pessimistic, there is no question that lots of variables come into play when undertaking a major project. The weather can play a factor. Maybe someone gets sick. Maybe materials are delayed.

You will need lots of patience and resilience. But the rewards can certainly be worth it.

Negotiation and Delegation Skills

Many, if not most, homeowners who become their own GC's put saving money at the top of their reasons for doing so. Being your own GC means that you will be hiring many different subcontractors and also buying all kinds of materials, fixtures, supplies, etc. As I've already said, you will need to ask Subs to bid on specific jobs. There could be hundreds of people qualified to do the job. Choose up to three Subs and have them give you a written estimate. (We'll talk more about choosing your Subs later.) You can use a Specification Sheet that outlines exactly what you want, and they will come back to you with the details on materials, costs, time frame, warranties, etc.

When you get your estimates, you will need to compare them and also see if the subcontractors can work across different parts of your project. For example, you can hire one electrician for your kitchen, bath, bedroom, etc. Or if your kitchen remodeler works closely with one electrician, you may hire that person for the kitchen and another for the bath, especially if the jobs are spread out over time. You want to make sure you have the right people for the specific jobs you need done.

Your ability to negotiate will depend on how knowledgeable you are about the jobs to be done and also what others are paying. Rates go up and down depending on availability, seasons, etc. Right now, there is something of a building boom, as many homeowners are putting in home offices or reconfiguring rooms for remote working.

Negotiation is an area that can only be touched upon here. If you're not someone who likes to bargain and involve yourself in give and take, one option is to hire someone for the role. They don't have to be a GC but rather someone who specializes in Procurement. Whatever you decide, you're going to have to make a lot of decisions involving money and how it is allocated. The good news is that you are essentially paying yourself to be the orchestra leader. Don't forget that you are not spending 20%-50% for overhead.

One thing about hiring and supervising the actual work that gets performed should be mentioned. Don't be a micro-manager, someone who is constantly looking over the shoulder of the people they hire. If you're working with competent and trustworthy people at a fair price that you've both agreed on, there's no need to be constantly monitoring them as they do their work. There's going to be an element of trust in the relationship. You need to treat them as the professionals they are. If they are not professional, you shouldn't hire them in the first place. Yes, you are the boss, but there are two parties (or more) involved. Hopefully, you have checked out the workmanship, reliability, and trustworthiness of your Subs before you hire them. You will save yourself from a lot of headaches.

The old saying from woodworking – "measure twice, cut once" – comes to mind. Evaluate thoroughly in advance and you will only need to hire once.

Now I'll show you how to be smart in your hiring process.

How to Be Smart About Hiring Subcontractors

As a GC, you don't need to know how to hammer a nail if you don't want to. In fact, you don't even need to know what a hammer is. That's the job of the subcontractor (tradesperson) you are going to hire. You are likely going to need lots of different specialists for different jobs. Here's a list of people you may require, depending on the project you want done:

- Cabinet maker
- Carpenter (Framing, roughing, finishing)
- Cleaning crew contractor
- Countertop contractor
- Drywall contractor
- Electrician
- Flooring and carpets
- Heating, ventilation, and air-conditioning (HVAC) contractor
- Insulation contractor
- Landscape contractor
- Licensed appraiser
- Mason
- Painter
- Plumber
- Roofer
- Tile contractor
- Waterproofing contractor

Of all of the above, your carpenter is likely to be the center of your project, as he or she needs to be there at the beginning and end. (You may have more than one carpenter involved, of course.) You can't very well put up drywall unless the frame has been built, and you can't make finishing touches until cabinets have been installed. Carpenters are likely to have several preferred vendors they do business with, and they often work with other subcontractors as a team. If you can find a reputable carpenter with an extended network, you can save yourself a lot of time.

Besides quality of workmanship, you will want to know about prices, payment terms, warranties, guarantees, references, recommendations, reputation, familiarity with local codes and authorities (inspectors), scheduling, etc. Common sense applies here. Most companies don't offer much of a warranty on their workmanship, and there are some who won't even return your call if something goes wrong. You want to look for value and someone you feel comfortable with. I can't give you advice here about your specific situation, but buyer beware.

Where to Find Subcontractors

Although there is no shortage of places to look for subcontractors online, you can start by seeking out contractors that offer the Premier Access Card in your area. They are affiliated with a trusted network of Subs they rely on day in and day out. You should also contact people in your personal network. If you know someone who has remodeled recently, ask them for recommendations. You may even be able to check out how well their experience was and the workmanship involved. You can also ask people in the industry that you trust. Visit home supply stores or a lumber yard and ask for advice. Most people are happy to talk freely, as they know that local homeowners are the lifeblood of their business. If no one is remodeling or building, they don't have a business.

You are looking for unbiased recommendations that fit your situation. Some Subs excel at simple jobs that don't take too long. If they were given a big complex project, they would be in over their head and likely headed for disaster. But they're not going to tell you that, and neither are many others.

Subcontractor Websites, Online Ratings and Rankings

Given the widespread use of the internet for almost all things under the sun, you can find all kinds of sites that showcase remodelers, contractors, subcontractors, tradespeople, etc. Listings and reviews are plentiful. The problem is that some of them are more trustworthy than others. You need to know who is paying whom, if anything, to be listed.

Every credible subcontractor is going to have his or her own website unless they are so busy that one isn't necessary. Their website is, or should be, a place where you can get a lot of information in order to narrow down the people you are going to contact for a bid.

Be sure to look at the references provided on subcontractor websites. Assuming that they are not fabricated (which has been known to happen, surprise, surprise), the more positive and plentiful the reviews, the better. Check out what clients say and look at the pictures of their jobs.

What about listings, ratings and rankings of suppliers and subcontractors located practically anywhere in North America by giving them a few details. And you might even get lucky by landing on someone or some store where you get a great deal. But you need to be careful. Many of these sites are pure advertising, even though they may present themselves as unbiased. In other words, the only people who show up on these sites are the ones who pay to be listed. There's nothing wrong with this – advertising is a valuable form of communication, and the phrase "it pays to advertise" has a lot of merit – but don't be fooled into thinking that you are getting an "unbiased" selection when companies show up on your search results. Whether a firm is reputable or reliable isn't the responsibility of the platform, although they may claim otherwise. If you want to have certainty, it is wise to do your research.

So, when you see "The Top 10 Carpenters" or "Top 10 Plumbers" in a local area, there may only be 10 carpenters and plumbers who have paid to be mentioned.

When all is said and done, you'll need to go out for bids. You don't want to call 10 plumbers, 10 electricians, 10 carpenters, and so on. If you do, you should probably hire a GC (or give me a call). Subcontractors look at your plans, listen to your ideas, and give you an estimate of the cost and timeline for your project. They figure out the moving parts, assemble them, schedule them, and get the work done. Generally speaking, they must be licensed, which means passing required exams and knowing building codes. Without a license, a subcontractor won't be able to pull the necessary building permits with local officials. Unless your project is tiny in scope, it's going to need to be inspected for safety and other reasons, and you want the job to be done on the up and up. (Never hire someone who won't pull a permit for "cost reasons" – it could come back to haunt you.)

Renovating, designing and building in Greater Toronto for over 40 years.
All workmanship guaranteed for life.

Which Pros Should You Hire?

Who should you hire? In terms of making your dreams a reality, the answer is, "it depends." Factors such as price and terms, your comfort level in dealing with the person and firm, their experience and reputation, who will be doing the actual work, and references need to be considered. Obviously, I don't know your specific circumstances, but here are some of the questions you should ask when you interview people. Don't forget that you may be spending months with them, so your intuition should play a part in your decision-making, not just the numbers.

- What kind of experience do you have with my type of project?

- How long have you been in business? Are you licensed and insured?

- What do you need to inspect in the existing structure to give us an estimate?

- Who will I be dealing with on a day-to-day basis?

- How do you determine cost and any unforeseen expenses?

- Where would my job fit with your schedule?

- Are you or members of your team certified by any organizations?

- What are your payment terms, and how much of a deposit is required? (You want to pay as you go along, as measured by meeting specific milestones. Deposits are sometimes capped by law, and you should check with your local licensing authorities.)

- How do you deal with change orders and allowances (overruns)?

- What kind of warranty or guarantee do you have?

- What percent of your business is repeat or referral business?

What are your local references? Can I see examples of jobs you have completed?

This is not a comprehensive list, and you will no doubt have many questions of your own. You need to feel comfortable with the firm and the person you are dealing with as well as their pricing, schedule, and their overall team. A renovation or remodeling job is a complex undertaking, often taking months to complete and dozens of people coming in and out of your home.

Common sense is the rule here. Check bids, references, warranties, workmanship, schedule, ease of doing business, etc. Insist upon a written contract that spells out the work to be performed, a schedule, materials used, etc. If you expect variances or allowances, make sure that they are capped ("not to exceed 10% of the fee quoted" is common) and not left open-ended.

Then make your decisions and get started. Don't forget, it's your money.

Before
Premier Quality Renovations

After
Premier Quality Renovations

Common Mistakes and How to Avoid Them

Having been in business for more than four decades, the horror stories I've seen or heard about would make Stephen King's hair stand on end. Jobs left unfinished, poor workmanship, using the wrong materials, code violations, kickbacks, the list goes on and on. These are for the most part avoidable. If you are going to be your own GC, you need to make sure you have your ducks lined up in order before you decide to tackle the job. You are ultimately responsible for making sure things go right. But you don't have to do it alone. Premier Renovation Consultants can be there right alongside you to guide you through every step of the process.

Let's cover some of the most common renovation mistakes made by owners who act as their own GC.

1. Not having your design in place.

If you are undertaking any kind of significant renovation, you are going to need designs or drawings with precise measurements so that you can order the right materials, allow your Subs to estimate and build accurately, and so on. Sometimes it's worth hiring an architect or interior designer to make sure you can accomplish the job you want. Unless you know what a load bearing wall is and how to do a workaround in case you want to remove it, you can find yourself in serious trouble. Professionals are trained to spot designs that won't work or are likely to lead to "buyer's remorse" later. What may look good on paper could prove to be difficult to live in. Inadequate or hard-to-access storage spaces are common. Who couldn't use another closet or part of the basement for those odds and ends that inevitably accumulate over time?

2. Not understanding the permitting and inspection process.

Even though you may not pull the permits yourself from local officials, you should understand the permitting and inspection process before you begin the actual work on your project. After all, you are going to be paying for the cost of permits and inspections, so you should know what is and is not allowed in your situation. You may not be zoned for the use you intend, or the addition you dreamed of may not conform to local codes. For example, many local zoning rules specify that there must be a minimum number of feet between property lines. You don't want to design an elaborate structure only to find that it is a code violation. I have seen lots of expensive work go up in smoke because of violations or because they won't pass inspection. Don't forget - ignorance is not an excuse and trying to obtain a variance or exemption could be a losing proposition. Contact our Premier Consulting Service or your local Building Office for guidance.

3. Mismanaging your schedule.
Juggling all the aspects of a renovation is a bit like putting together a jigsaw puzzle where the pieces may be in flux. Certain parts of the job can be done simultaneously, while other parts need to be done sequentially. If you are ordering kitchen cabinets, they can be built when the project starts, but they can't be installed until the electrical and framing have taken place. You know what I mean. There are various scheduling programs that will allow you to see how your timeline changes depending on which tasks depend on others and which don't. As the GC, you need to have an organized checklist in place to help keep on top of the project flow.

4. Failure to get everyone to work together.
Scheduling and coordination problems can lead to costly delays, and this could have ramifications for your entire project. A job that was supposed to be completed a week ago but slips into an unknown future date can have a domino effect. Your Subs will build some slack into their schedules, but they are on a timeline and are likely to be working more than one job at a time. If you miss a "window of opportunity," you could find yourself up a creek without a paddle. You need lots of cooperation and coordination, and if you aren't the type who can work with lots of people at the same time and keep everything in order, you may want to hire someone specifically devoted to this task.

5. Failing to anticipate time and cost overruns.
John Lennon said that "life happens while you're busy making other plans." In the movie Forrest Gump, "it happens" is featured in a prominent scene. In other words, life seldom goes according to plan. Renovations are no exception. You need to prepare for the unexpected. If you plan on moving out of your house while your bedrooms are being renovated, you should anticipate being

away for more than you bargained for – just in case. Or if your kitchen will be unusable for a period, expect that the job will take longer than you scheduled. Making arrangements ahead of time will alleviate unnecessary stress.

Time and cost overruns can be due to factors beyond your control. Tearing down a wall could expose rotting beams that need to be replaced. Or you may find that the insulation you had put in no longer gives you the protection you need. Being flexible will help you get out of a lot of jams. And of course, having the money to pay for extra costs should be built into your budget.

6. Running out of money.

Let's face it – things often cost more than you expect. And the unexpected, which we've just covered, is to be expected. If you've set aside a specific amount for your renovation, you may have to scale back or leave certain tasks incomplete if you overspend during the early phases of your project. More than once I've seen a homeowner run out of funds before their project was complete, which meant that things didn't get done. It's one thing to have a temporary inconvenience but it's another to leave a job incomplete for an extended period. Building a cushion into your budget will help with the unforeseen. Not everyone responds well to uncertainty, especially when your lifestyle is at stake.

7. Changing your mind along the way.

Although everyone has the right to change one's mind as time goes by, it's another thing to change plans midstream. I'm not talking about the colour of your paint, of course, but about major things like the placement of fixtures, the number of light switches to be installed, or how many cabinets you want.

Change can be complicated or simple. You want to avoid "change orders" that will result in delays or increased costs. The latter is sometimes a license to overbill, especially if time is involved. What was supposed to take a week may run into weeks if too many variables are involved.

8. Not giving enough thought how you will live in your new space.

When you are designing your dream space, you need to consider what are often called human factors. How will the area be used? How will people move about the room? Is there enough space for the number of people you anticipate?

Kitchens have become the center of the modern household, and often they open into a dining room and/or family room. You don't want people to be cramped in their own living space. There are guidelines available from designers and architects that can help you maximize the amount of space you have and make it more functional. After the renovation is done, you will be enjoying your new creation for years to come. You want to make sure that it is designed to accommodate you, your family, and your friends.

9. Choosing a Sub without checking references.

You may find lots of people giving you recommendations on which plumber or electrician or carpenter to use. Maybe they had a good experience or heard about someone who did. However, you should check their references and maybe ask around at the local building supply store or housing authority. Good Subs are not afraid of their reputation and are happy to have people spread the word, but not-so-good Subs may have something to hide. If you do enough homework, you should be able to separate the wheat from the chaff. You may find that you have to wait a bit to hire the person(s) you want, but it may be worth it. You will see their fruits of their efforts long after they have departed to the next job.

10. Believing you are getting a "special deal."

Some Subs may offer you a "special deal" to get the job. This could be a price concession, a good deal on supplies, or any number of "for you today only" deals. Sometimes these are legitimate, but often they are not.

The phrase "you get what you pay for" applies a lot of the time, and if you go for what seems to be a "bargain," you could end up with a substandard job. I can't count the number of times I have been called in to fix someone else's work, it's not uncommon. Check out all offers thoroughly if you have the time. Obviously, you are not in a great bargaining position if your roof is leaking, but you typically have options. Buyer beware.

11. Not knowing which questions to ask or not speaking up enough.

A lot of homeowners are more trusting than they should be, especially when it comes to the remodeling industry. We defer to experts, so if a plumber tells you that your water pump needs to be replaced, you are likely to believe him or her.

It's human nature. However, for any significant job that can wait, it could be worth getting a second opinion. In fact, some in the trade recommend that you get three bids for every job (unless you already know and trust someone). I once heard about someone who was having water pressure problems. The plumber did some adjustments to the pressurizer and fixed the issue. His office did not quite get the message that the problem had been solved, and someone called the homeowner and told them that they needed a new tank. This would have cost the homeowner more than a thousand dollars.

It pays to ask questions, even if they may seem intrusive. Good Subs like to work with knowledgeable homeowners and are not out to take advantage of anyone. On the other hand, don't micromanage and try to tell people how to do their job. There's a reason why professionals have licenses and formal education in their respective fields. If you feel uncomfortable with someone or sense that you are being unduly pressured, it's your right to walk away.

12. Delivering final payments too early.

Your final payment is the leverage you have when the job is done. Subs want to be paid right away, as they, like the rest of us, have bills to pay. And a dollar today is worth more than a dollar tomorrow. However, your contract should specify a payment schedule. Don't rush to pay the last amount, especially if you haven't inspected the work.

Have a Punch List broken down by each subcontractor. This is a detailed list of small items that still need to be addressed and completed before final approval and can be a necessary incentive to have any loose ends tied up. Contact your Premier Renovation Consultant for a site visit prior to final inspection and releasing of any payment.

It may take a bit of time to make sure everything is in order, and you want to be dealing with people whose lives do not depend on your payment. Everyone might get into a pinch now and then, but good Subs have plenty of work lined up and are not desperate for the next job.

How do you avoid the common mistakes we've just talked about? A lot of them can be prevented by good planning, but life doesn't always go according to plan. Your resourcefulness and ability to improvise will no doubt be tested, so you should cultivate flexibility and adaptability. If you are a rigid person and easily upset when things don't go your way, being your own GC may not be right for you.

However, don't forget that expert help is always available. Peter and Premier's team work with people all over the world, and thanks to technological innovations, we can see what you see. You don't have to do it alone; we will guide you through the complete process to a successful completion.

To arrange a call on the following platforms:

please contact us at

info@premier-renovations.com

www.premier-renovations.com

1-905-286-0303

Getting the Most for Your Money

Whether we are looking for a luxury makeover or a less expensive upgrade, we all want to get a good deal. In order for you to get the best value for your money, here are some guidelines.

Advance planning is the key to success. If you start thinking about your dream project early enough, you may be able to find fixtures and supplies on sale long before they will be needed. Many stores have clearance sales or holiday specials on a regular basis, and you can stock up at a fraction of the cost of retail prices. You may even find bargains on Craigslist or other sites.

Have an overview of your entire project well before getting estimates from the subcontractors who will do the work. You will often need to have them perform their work in a specific order, with carpenters often the first (and sometimes last) to be on the job. As I said before, you are like an orchestra leader, and you will be directing each section of the orchestra to play at the right time. It is hard to be organized when you are still planning in the midst of a job. I've seen this happen too many times, and the result is often a job that costs more and takes longer than originally anticipated. Making changes to your plans while the job is in progress is often a recipe for skyrocketing costs.

Seek at least three bidders unless you know them well or unless you are given a quality referral from someone you trust (not someone who knows someone). For example, carpenters often work with a small circle of plumbers or electricians, since their work often dovetails. If your carpenter recommends someone who seems qualified and competitive, choosing them could save you a lot of interviewing time that can be spent elsewhere. Make sure everyone who bids has a specification sheet you give to them to complete so that the bids are apples to apples comparisons.

Don't pay subcontractors in cash. Use a credit card, cheque, or money transfer and get a receipt for your payment. Keep a binder dedicated to financials and organize your receipts. You need to have a paper trail. In the case of a dispute, your credit card company may be able to intervene to help settle matters.

Don't pay the final subcontractor installment until you are completely satisfied with the work and have it inspected by your local Premier Consultant.

Don't jump at the low bidder. Think value rather than price. The low bidder may be the best for the job, but they may also skimp on materials or use inferior parts. Make sure you have a written contract that spells out the details of the work to be performed and firm prices rather than estimates. As I said, you can build in a +10% for "allowances" much like an automobile shop will quote you a price plus a small overrun before they need additional approval. It may be that when a wall is exposed or old fixtures removed, problems that could not be seen in advance will surface. Of course, you will want them fixed even though it will cost more than you had anticipated.

"WELL, THEY WERE THE LOW BIDDERS."

Beware of anyone who offers a "buy now" special or who puts undue pressure on you. You need to be the judge of this, of course, and there may be very good reasons for buying sooner rather than later. Sometimes there are limited quantities of the latest appliances or the newest materials, and it could be worth taking advantage of them. You are looking for a good and fair deal, and they can be had in any number of ways.

See if you can get special pricing on appliances, fixtures, and supplies from your Premier Access Card or a local Premier Authorized Contractor.

Make sure that clean-up is built into your contracts. You don't want to be stuck with lots of debris and waste. Your home should be left in what is called "broom clean" condition.

Obtain a "firm" estimate of the time required for completion, knowing that disruptions can and do take place. You will be juggling the schedules of several different Subs, and often the work of one will depend on the work of another. You can't install new cabinets until framing and drywall have been done.

Determine the subcontractor's "communications style" before making your decision. How fast someone responds and how thorough they are when you ask questions should give you a good idea of how easy they will be to work with. Not everyone is a match for everyone else, or as the saying goes, "you can't please everyone all of the time." Sometimes there won't be a match due to personality rather than competence. In such cases, it is better to look elsewhere.

Ask yourself if the subcontractor presents himself or herself professionally. There is no need for a man to wear a jacket and tie or a woman to dress up, but sloppy dress and appearance often translates into the same type of work.

Beware of anyone who asks you to pull permits. This could signal that they don't have the necessary license or that they are not in good standing with local officials. If they are on the up and up, there should be no problem with having them procure the necessary paperwork and inspections.

Watch out for what those in the industry call "professional padding," especially if you live in an upscale, high income area. Doctors, lawyers, stockbrokers, executives, and other professionals who live in "exclusive" towns or neighbourhoods are often quoted prices higher than others simply because they appear to be able to afford it. You may be able to find out from others what the "going rate" is for your type of work and eliminate any surcharge.

Beware of anyone who shows up at your door with "extra materials" from a job down the street that you can buy for a song. And watch out for door-to-door handymen looking for odd jobs. If it sounds too good to be true, it often is.

Check references thoroughly. In addition to looking at examples of completed jobs, ask your local building officials for recommendations and the "inside scoop." You may also find that local hardware stores can give you unbiased recommendations. Contact us for your local Premier Certified Contractor.

Make sure that your own insurance will cover Subs who may be injured on the job or the like. Sometimes liability isn't clear, and their insurance and bonding may be inadequate. Your insurance agent will be able to tell you whether you need special coverage during your construction.

Don't forget to treat your Subs as professionals. If they have treated you fairly, give them a good recommendation if asked for. References are a key source of business for many of them, and there is no need to be stingy when asked for help. Of course, if you had a bad experience, you have every right to say so.

How to Buy Wholesale Like A Pro and Save Thousands

The materials you use in your renovation can be a sizable portion of your overall budget, so you want to get the best value you can. If you can save money here or there, you may be able to afford a higher quality refrigerator or an extra closet instead of having to settle for less. Your appliances, cabinets, furniture, rugs, lamps, patio, etc. are all going to be lived in, whereas labour and workmanship will fade into the background (assuming that the work is up to standard). Keep that in mind as you think about how you will be living in the spaces you are building.

Markups charged by GC's and Subs tend to be from 20%-50%. In other words, you will be paying $120 to $150 at retail, whereas they can buy the goods for $100. Contractors are essentially acting on behalf of the manufacturer. It is their job to ensure quality. If you are the buyer, that's your responsibility.

Contractors and subcontractors have special relationships with local and national suppliers that allow them to buy at wholesale rather than retail. "Professional discounts" are available depending on the kind of relationship the buyer has with the seller, but purchasing volume is a key consideration. If you buy lumber by the truckload instead of a few boards at a time, you will get a better price.

Premier Quality Renovations has close relationships with trusted suppliers and subcontractors. We have vetted each and every one of them and can buy at up to 60% off retail. Now we offer the Premier Access Card to anyone who wants to save money on both materials and labour. You can find more details below.

Even if you do not live in the Toronto area, Premier Quality Renovations has launched the Premier Certified Network, a network of GC's across North America who offer a local version of the Premier Access Card, consulting services, and other benefits. You will be able to find good discounts through the network to maximize your savings on your renovation.

And don't forget that as the GC who knows the entire project from top to bottom, including the schedule, you may be able to purchase goods months before they will be needed. Just as car models go out of style at the end of the model year and are heavily discounted, there are regular closeouts and special deals on everything from bathroom fixtures to appliances to heating systems to air conditioners. Assuming that your financing allows it, you can take advantage of such special deals and save yourself thousands of dollars. You can even set up your phone to give you alerts when prices change. That way, you will be notified when good deals come around. It pays to shop around.

Premier Has Been Featured on These Trusted News Sources

About Premier Quality Renovations

Premier Quality Renovations offers three lines of business:

1. Renovation Services

Building a successful renovation and design business for 41 years isn't built on luck – but on word-of-mouth, reputation and exceptional skills. Premier Quality Renovations can take your project from the idea stage to final project completion. We work with architects, engineers, design specialists, and others to ensure that your project is exactly what you want. Trained in the old-school way, we know that shortcuts usually lead to more expense and disappointment. We offer a lifetime guarantee on our workmanship, so we need to get it done right the first time. In addition, we don't ask for much of a deposit compared to some other firms.

Before
Premier Quality Renovations

After
Premier Quality Renovations

Christian's Home

Before Renovation

After Renovation

Premier

QUALITY RENOVATIONS

Before
Premier Quality Renovations

After
Premier Quality Renovations

"Trust is a big factor. We don't take upfront fees. We work with the client to ensure they are comfortable with respect to the work and a customized payment schedule."

We also charge you the same price we pay for materials and supplies. There is no need for us to mark anything up. We believe in a pay-as-you go policy, meaning that we have a stake in the project like you do. We know that we will be paid when the job is complete, so there is no need to stick you with a huge bill in advance. That is one of the reasons why my growing team of experienced tradespeople produce professional results that meet deadlines and expectations.

We offer three unique payment options under Renovation Services

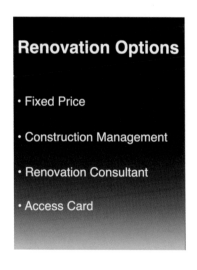

Renovation Options

- Fixed Price

- Construction Management

- Renovation Consultant

- Access Card

Fixed Price Option

This standard payment option is typical for small to medium sized projects and guarantees you a fixed price. Choosing this option, there are no unexpected surprises which can sometimes arise during a renovation project. You can be confident in knowing how much you need to budget for your project.

Management Fee Option

This unique payment option which is typically reserved for larger projects is based on the combined cost of the materials and labour required to complete the project plus a 20% management fee. It reflects the true total cost of the project, therefore providing you with considerable cost savings as opposed to choosing the fixed price option.

Consulting Service Option

This payment option is ideal if you prefer to be your own GC. You oversee the whole renovation process yourself with the assurance and confidence of working with an experienced Premier building renovation consultant, giving you complete control over cost, quality and type of materials and labour used for the projects. We are on call virtually (Zoom, WebEx) and onsite from anywhere in North America through our Premier Certified Network.

FIXED PRICE OPTION	MANAGEMENT FEE	CONSULTING SERVICE
This standard payment option is typical for small to medium sized projects and guarantees you a fixed price. Choosing this option, there are no unexpected surprises which can sometimes arise during a renovation project. You can be confident in knowing how much you need to budget for your project.	This unique payment option which is typically reserved for larger projects is based on the combined cost of the materials and labour required to complete the project plus a 20% management fee and reflects the true total cost of the project, therefore providing you with considerable cost savings as opposed to choosing the fixed price option.	This payment option is ideal if you prefer to be your own DIY general contractor. You oversee the whole renovation process yourself with the assurance and confidence of working with an experienced Premier building renovation consultant, giving you complete control over cost, quality and type of materials and labour used for the projects.

1. Premier Quality Home Inspections

Premier Quality Inspections are designed to help you eliminate costly mistakes and bad decisions before you purchase your new home. For a low one-time fee, Premier will be your buying advisor and inform you whether or not your renovation goals are achievable and cost efficient, taking into account the value of the home.

Looking to convert the kitchen to an open concept? Or perhaps you want to build your dream suite or bathroom. You need to know what's going on where you can't see. Don't buy before you know! Premier's experienced inspection team will analyze the feasibility of your plan and will advise you on the best approach on achieving your renovation goal. We are not beholden to a real estate agent or a bank, so we can give our independent opinion. We can also obtain a price estimate from our network right on the spot!

All this for a service fee starting at $500 can save you money and hassles down the road. The best part is that if you decide to hire Premier Quality Renovations for the job, we will rebate the inspection fee!

Premier's inspection teams have extensive backgrounds in construction and renovations. They know where to look for building problems that will cause future issues or affect the value of the house.

2. Renovation Consulting (Online or Onsite)

This service of Premier Quality Renovations reaches out to homeowners planning renovations who basically know what they want but seek the backup of experienced consultation for the process. Now, with Premier Renovation Consultants you can buy that confidence. For $500 per site visit, you can get expert advice on renovation steps, scheduling and inspection of the work done. It's a bit like hiring a flight instructor to help you fly an airplane. You could never learn to fly from reading a manual alone; you need someone guiding you as you take controls of the airplane and actually fly the plane. Similarly, if you tried to be your own GC with only book learning as training, you'll likely run into problems.

Instead, you can rely on Premier's Consultants, or instructors, who will assist you every step of the way. They'll give you the knowledge and confidence needed to make your renovation project a success. That's a small investment to make to avoid costly missteps on your renovation project that will likely run into tens or hundreds of thousands of dollars. Better still, if you go with Premier Quality Renovations to handle a project over $10,000, we will rebate the initial consulting fee.

We can be your online partner in completing your home improvements or renovations. Homeowners can execute their projects just as if your contractor were right beside you, guiding you through every step of the renovation process. With your smartphone or laptop, we can be looking over your shoulder, guiding you every step of the way.

3. Premier Access Card

To Get Your Access Card - Go to www.premier-renovations.com/access

Now you can save thousands on your reno across North America no matter who does your renovation. Keeping money in your pocket has never been easier thanks to the one-of-a-kind Premier Access Card. Renovations are known to be expensive, but with the help of the Premier Access Card, homeowners are granted access to an elite referral network of hundreds of Premier's reputable and trusted suppliers and trades in the Greater Toronto Area and others in major cities across North America. Card holders are entitled to wholesale pricing up to 60% off, which means big savings.

This unique card is the only one of its kind in North America, and makes a big difference when it comes to planning your home building projects. Many people struggle when it comes to their renovations because they don't know who to hire, how to find the suppliers they want, or how much to pay. This card gives you complete access to a comprehensive list of industry professionals that we have personally worked with and recommend. The wholesale pricing offers such steep discounts that most of our clients have saved tens of thousands of dollars on their projects.

The Premier Access Card is offered in conjunction with Premier's Renovation Consultants, both of which are designed to help you consult, design, build and renovate your home. Looking to start a renovation but unsure as to what is required? Premier's experienced consultants can get you started down the right path – perfect for homeowners who want to oversee the renovation process but want the assurance and confidence of working with an experienced building renovation consultant.

The Premier Access Card gives you an "A-to-Z" listing of everything you could need when it comes to turning your house into your dream home. Just a few of the many categories we cover:

Carpenters	Appliances
Electricians	Bath Fixtures
Engineers	Drywall
Flooring	Contractors Lighting
HVAC	Mirrors
Plumbers	Tiling
Roofers	Windows and Doors

Give Premier a call today to find out how we can help you with your next dream project.

1-905-286-0303

info@premier-renovations.com

www.premier-renovations.com

A Few of Our Awards and Certifications.
See www.premier-renovations.com for more.

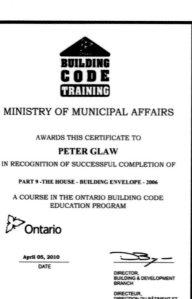

MINISTRY OF MUNICIPAL AFFAIRS

AWARDS THIS CERTIFICATE TO

PETER GLAW

IN RECOGNITION OF SUCCESSFUL COMPLETION OF

PART 9 -THE HOUSE - BUILDING ENVELOPE - 2006

A COURSE IN THE ONTARIO BUILDING CODE
EDUCATION PROGRAM

Ontario

April 05, 2010
DATE

DIRECTOR,
BUILDING & DEVELOPMENT
BRANCH

DIRECTEUR,
DIRECTION DU BÂTIMENT ET
DE L'AMENAGEMENT

Certificate of Completion

On behalf of EnerQuality, this certificate recognizes

Peter Glaw

for successfully completing

Part 9 Air Barrier/Air Tightness

Date: May 28, 2019   Instructor: Andy Oding
Location: Toronto, Ontario   Workshop length: 420 minutes

Certificate of Completion

On behalf of EnerQuality, this certificate recognizes

Peter Glaw

for successfully completing

Advanced Building Science

Date: May 12 & 13, 2020   Instructor: Andy Oding
Location: Toronto, Ontario   Workshop length: 360 minutes

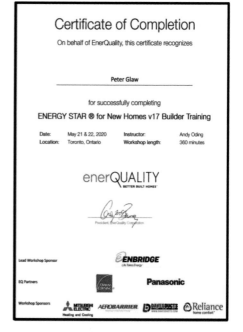

Certificate of Completion

On behalf of EnerQuality, this certificate recognizes

Peter Glaw

for successfully completing

ENERGY STAR ® for New Homes v17 Builder Training

Date: May 21 & 22, 2020   Instructor: Andy Oding
Location: Toronto, Ontario   Workshop length: 360 minutes

What Clients Say

What Clients Say About Premier Quality Renovations

"I am so happy with my new bathrooms! I would like to thank Peter and his on-site crew Mario and Stan for the superb reno performed on my 2 condo bathrooms in Jan/20. The entire experience was top notch from the initial planning, the demolition, the reconstruction and the finishing. Peter's estimate of time required for the job was accurate. Every construction jobsite creates dust/dirt and my condo was no different but the difference with my job was Peter and his folks minimized the dirt/dust by covering the furniture the floors with plastic before the job started The crew performed a full cleaning at the end of every construction day. Keeping my condo was especially important to me since I had to live in the condo throughout the construction. I had no complaints with the dust/dirt level during construction. Long story short, Peter really cares about doing the best he can for you from day 1 to the end of the job and beyond. You will not go wrong having Peter handle your reno."   *Laurie*

Christian's Home

Before Renovation

After Renovation

"Premier offers lifetime warranty on their work and that gave us a lot of confidence on the Genuity of the business."

Christian & Sheila, Toronto

Before
Premier Renovations

After
Premier Renovations

"We met Peter Glaw from Premier Renovations when he was working on a project in our area and soon Peter was walking through our old house.

If you are looking for a contractor or company and a great group of people Peter and his team are who you would want for your project. They are dedicated, professional, on time and give valuable suggestions throughout the whole process. We truly enjoyed working with everyone on this project.

We are thrilled with our new home and although it's an open concept it still exudes a very welcoming feeling when you step inside. Seeing is believing, so check out the before and after photos. This was a real transformation.

Every day we walk through the front door we feel the warmth and coziness and it will always remind us of the dedication and determination that was put into this project by everyone. Everyone put heart and soul into this project, and we cannot thank you enough. Congratulations to all who worked on this project and made it happen. We are over the moon and so happy to be back in our brand-new home.

We highly recommend Peter Glaw and his team for a stellar performance indeed.

Note: Mario and Stan — thank you for the great conversations and cappuccinos we shared. We miss that for sure and we wish you well with all your projects in the future. You guys are amazing!"

Johan and Erica

Before
Premier Renovations

After
Premier Renovations

"Premier is always available and on the job all the time."

Johan & Erica, Port Credit

"Premier recently completed our entire basement renovation and totally exceeded our expectations."

Nancy & Tim, Oakville

"Premier's Access Card saved us $150K on our $820K renovation project!"

Pat & Danielle, Toronto

Tables & Charts

In the following pages there is space after each chart or table for you to add your own notes or calculations. In the budget section you may want to record your receipts here for quick reference.

ESTIMATING & BUDGETING WORKSHEET

Description	Estimated Cost	Actual Cost	Amount Paid
GENERAL REQUIREMENTS			
Construction Project Consultant			
Architect			
Engineer			
Survey			
Insurance			
Financing costs			
Legal fees			
Other			
Subtotal			

Description	Estimated Cost	Actual Cost	Amount Paid
SITE PREPERATION			
Safety equipment			
Demolition			
Jacking & Shoring			
Garbage bin and removal			
Portable toilet			
Temp power			
Temp heat			
Scaffolding rental			
Equipment/ tool rental			
Other			
Subtotal			

Description	Estimated Cost	Actual Cost	Amount Paid
UTILITIES			
Water			
Sewer			
Electrical, Permit			
Gas, Permit			
Other			
Subtotal			

Description	Estimated Cost	Actual Cost	Amount Paid
EXCAVATION			
Foundation excavation			
Backfill			
Finish grading			
Landscaping			
Other			
Subtotal			

Description	Estimated Cost	Actual Cost	Amount Paid
FOUNDATION			
Footings			
Steel reinforcing			
Foundation walls			
Sub-slab vapor barrier			
Basement, garage concrete floor			
Sump pump			
Foundation windows			
Waterproofing			
Foundation drain board			
Slab insulation			
Exterior foundation insulation			
Other			
Subtotal			

Description	Estimated Cost	Actual Cost	Amount Paid
OTHER MASONRY, PAVING			
Patios			
Exterior stairs			
Masonry chimneys			
Fireplaces			
Driveway			
Walkways			
Other			
Subtotal			

Description	Estimated Cost	Actual Cost	Amount Paid
FRAMING			
Trusses and roof			
Rough framing carpentry			
Other			
Subtotal			

Description	Estimated Cost	Actual Cost	Amount Paid
ROOFING			
Roof underlayment, shingles			
Gutters and downspouts			
Skylights			
Other			
Subtotal			

Description	Estimated Cost	Actual Cost	Amount Paid
EXTERIOR			
Exterior sheathing			
Weather barrier (Tyvek, etc.)			
Membrane and flashing			
Brick, stone, stucco, siding etc.			
Fascia, soffit			
Other exterior trim			
Exterior stairs, landing			
Exterior paint, stain, caulking			
Other			
Subtotal			

Description	Estimated Cost	Actual Cost	Amount Paid
WINDOWS & EXTERIOR DOORS			
Windows			
Doors			
Window & door hardware			
Other			
Subtotal			

Description	Estimated Cost	Actual Cost	Amount Paid
PLUMBING			
Plumbing rough in			
Sump pump, backwater valve			
Water heater			
Plumbing fixtures			
Finish plumbing and installs			
Other			
Subtotal			

Description	Estimated Cost	Actual Cost	Amount Paid
ELECTRICAL			
Service panel, sub-panels			
Rough in wiring			
Phone, cable, internet wiring			
Light fixtures			
Exterior lighting			
Devices, outlets, switches,			
Home theater/entertainment			
Other			
Subtotal			

Description	Estimated Cost	Actual Cost	Amount Paid
HVAC			
Furnace/heat pump			
Central AC			
Air handler			
Radiators			
House ventilation, ERV, HRV			
Other			
Subtotal			

Description	Estimated Cost	Actual Cost	Amount Paid
INSULATION AND AIR SEALING			
Insulation, vapour barrier			
Eco spray foam insulation			
Other			
Subtotal			

Description	Estimated Cost	Actual Cost	Amount Paid
DRYWALL/PLASTER			
Drywall			
Crown moldings etc.			
Other			
Subtotal			

Description	Estimated Cost	Actual Cost	Amount Paid
INTERIOR FINISH			
Interior doors			
Door knobs, hardware			
Interior trim, baseboards, casing			
Built-in shelving, cabinets			
Closet shelving, hardware			
Stairs & railings			
Interior painting, staining			
Flooring, wood, tile, carpet			
Other flooring			
Other interior finish			
Interior carpentry			
Other			
Subtotal			

Description	Estimated Cost	Actual Cost	Amount Paid
KITCHEN & BATH			
Kitchen cabinets			
Bathroom cabinets			
Cabinet pulls, hardware			
Countertops, backsplash			
Tile, stone			
Shower doors/enclosure			
Mirrors			
Towel bar & accessories			
Other			
Subtotal			

Description	Estimated Cost	Actual Cost	Amount Paid
PORCHES AND DECKS			
Open porch			
Screened porch			
Wood or composite deck			
Fencing			
Other			
Subtotal			

Description	Estimated Cost	Actual Cost	Amount Paid
APPLIANCES			
Refrigerator			
Range, cooktop			
Microwave			
Range hood			
Dishwasher			
Washer/dryer			
Other			
Subtotal			
TOTAL CONSTRUCTION COSTS			

Metric Conversion Chart

WHEN THE MEASUREMENT GIVEN IS	TO CONVERT IT TO	MULTIPLY IT BY
Inches	Centimeters	2.54
Feet	Meters	0.305
Miles	Kilometers	1.6
Square Feet	Square Meters	0.0929
Cubic Yards	Cubic Meters	0.765
Pounds	Kilograms	0.45
°F	°C	°F − 32 x 5/9

Common Board Sizes

NORMAL SIZE	ACTUAL SIZE
1X2	¾" X 1½"
1X3	¾" X 2½"
1X4	¾" X 3½"
1X6	¾" X 5½"
1X8	¾"X 7¼"
2X2	1½" X 1½"
2X4	1½" X 3½"
2X6	1½" X 5½"
2X8	1½" X 7¼"
4X4	3½" X 3½"
6X6	5½" X 5½"

Metric Conversion Charts

Metric Length Conversions

1 centimeter	=	10 millimeters	1 cm	=	10 mm
1 decimeter	=	10 centimeters	1 dm	=	10 cm
1 meter	=	100 centimeters	1 m	=	100 cm
1 meter	=	10 decimeters	1 m	=	10 dm
1 kilometer	=	1000 meters	1 km	=	1000 m

Metric Liquid Volume (Capacity) Conversions

1 centiliter	=	10 milliliters	1 cl	=	10 ml
1 deciliter	=	10 centiliters	1 dl	=	10 cl
1 liter	=	1000 milliliters	1 l	=	1000 ml
1 liter	=	10 deciliters	1 l	=	10 dl
1 kiloliter	=	1000 liters	1 kl	=	1000 l

Metric Area Conversions

1 sq. centimeter	=	100 sq. millimeters	1 sq. cm	=	100 sq. mm
1 sq. meter	=	10,000 sq. centimeters	1 sq. m	=	10,000 sq. cm
1 hectare	=	10,000 sq. meters	1 ha	=	10,000 sq. m
1 sq. km	=	100 hectares	1 sq. km	=	100 ha
1 sq. km	=	1 million sq. meters	1 sq. km	=	1,000,000 sq. m

Metric Volume Conversions					
1 cubic centimeter	=	10,000 cubic millimeters	1 cu cm	=	1000 cu mm
1 cubic decimeter	=	1000 cubic centimeters	1 cu dm	=	1000 cu cm
1 cubic meter	=	1 million cubic centimeters	1 cu m	=	1,000,000 cu cm
1 cubic meter	=	1000 cubic centimeters	1 cu m	=	1000 cu dm

Metric Weight Conversions

1 gram	=	1000 milligrams	1 g	=	1000 mg
1 decagram	=	10 grams	1 dag	=	10 g
1 kilogram	=	1000 grams	1 kg	=	1000 g
1 tonne (1 megagram)	=	1000 kilograms	1 tonne (1 Mg)	=	1000 kg
1 gigagram	=	1000 megagrams	1 Gg	=	1000 Mg

Glossary

The following terms are commonly used in remodeling and new construction. They are used with permission from Home Building Manual. For a more comprehensive list of terms contact Premier Quality Renovations.

A/C - An abbreviation for air conditioner or air conditioning.

Allowance(s) - A sum of money set aside in the construction contract for items which have not been selected and specified in the construction contract. For example, selection of tile as a flooring may require an allowance for an underlayment material, or an electrical allowance which sets aside an amount of money to be spent on electrical fixtures.

Appraisal - An expert valuation of property.

Architect - One who has completed a course of study in building and design and is licensed by the state as an architect. One who draws up plans.

Back Charge - Billings for work performed or costs incurred by one party that, in accordance with the agreement, should have been performed or incurred by the party to whom billed. Owners bill back charges to general contractors, and general contractors bill back charges to subcontractors. Examples of back charges include charges for cleanup work or to repair something damaged by another subcontractor, such as a tub chip or broken window.

Bay Window - Any window space projecting outward from the walls of a building, either square or polygonal in plan.

Beam - A structural member transversely supporting a load. A structural member carrying building loads (weight) from one support to another. Sometimes called a "girder".

Bearing partition - A partition that supports any vertical load in addition to its own weight.

Bearing point - A point where a bearing or structural weight is concentrated and transferred to the foundation.

Bearing wall - A wall that supports any vertical load in addition to its own weight.

Bid - A formal offer by a contractor, in accordance with specifications for a project, to do all or a phase of the work at a certain price in accordance with the terms and conditions stated in the offer.

Bid shopping - A practice by which contractors, both before and after their bids are submitted, attempt to obtain prices from potential subcontractors and material suppliers that are lower than the contractors' original estimates on which their bids are based, or after a contract is awarded, seek to induce subcontractors to reduce the subcontract price included in the bid.

Bidding requirements - The procedures and conditions for the submission of bids. The requirements are included ion documents, such as the notice to bidders, advertisements for bids, instructions to bidders, invitations to bid, and sample bid forms.

Bifold door - Doors that are hinged in the middle for opening in a smaller area than standard swing doors. Often used for closet doors.

Binder - A receipt for a deposit to secure the right to purchase a home at an agreed term by a buyer and seller.

Bipass doors - Doors that slide by each other and commonly used as closet doors.

Blankets - Fiber-glass or rock-wool insulation that comes in long rolls 15 or 23 inches wide.

Blocked (door blocking) - Wood shims used between the door frame and the vertical structural wall framing members.

Blocked (rafters) - Short "2 by 4's" used to keep rafters from twisting and installed at the ends and at mid-span.

Blocking - Small wood pieces to brace framing members or to provide a nailing base for gypsum board or paneling.

Block out - To install a box or barrier within a foundation wall to prevent the concrete from entering an area. For example, foundation walls are sometimes "blocked" in order for mechanical pipes to pass through the wall, to install a crawl space door, and to depress the concrete at a garage door location.

Blow insulation - Fiber insulation in loose form and used to insulate attics and existing walls where framing members are not exposed.

Blueprint(s) - A type of copying method often used for architectural drawings. Usually used to describe the drawing of a structure which is prepared by an architect or designer for the purpose of design and planning, estimating, securing permits and actual construction.

Breaker panel - The electrical box that distributes electric power entering the home to each branch circuit (each plug and switch) and composed of circuit breakers.

Builder's Risk Insurance - Insurance coverage on a construction project during construction, including extended coverage that may be added for the contract for the customer's protections.

Building codes - Community ordinances governing the manner in which a home may be constructed or modified.

Building insurance - Insurance covering the structure of the building.

Caulking - (1) A flexible material used to seal a gap between two surfaces e.g. between pieces of siding or the corners in tub walls. (2) To fill a joint with mastic or asphalt plastic cement to prevent leaks.

CFM (cubic feet per minute) - A rating that expresses the amount of air a blower or fan can move. The volume of air (measured in cubic feet) that can pass through an opening in one minute.

Change order - A written document which modifies the plans and specifications and/or the price of the construction Contract.

Circuit Breaker - A device which looks like a switch and is usually located inside the electrical breaker panel or circuit breaker box. It is designed to (1) shut of the power to portions or all of the house and (2) to limit the amount of power flowing through a circuit (measured in amperes). 110-volt household circuits require a fuse or circuit breaker with a rating of 15 or a maximum of 20 amps. 220-volt circuits may be designed for higher amperage loads e.g. a hot water heater may be designed for a 30-amp load and would therefore need a 30-amp fuse or breaker.

Class "C" - Minimum fire rating issued by the Underwriters' Laboratories for roofing materials.

Clean out - An opening providing access to a drain line. Closed with a threaded plug.

Clip ties - Sharp, cut metal wires that protrude out of a concrete foundation wall (that at one time held the foundation form panels in place).

Cold air return - The ductwork (and related grills) that carries room air back to the furnace for re-heating.

Collar - Preformed flange placed over a vent pipe to seal the roofing above the vent pipe opening. Also called a vent sleeve.

Collar beam - Nominal 1 - or 2-inch-thick members connecting opposite roof rafters. They serve to stiffen the roof structure.

Column - A vertical structural compression member which supports loads.

Combustion air - The duct work installed to bring fresh, outside air to the furnace and/or hot water heater. Normally 2 separate supplies of air are brought in: One high and One low.

Combustion chamber - The part of a boiler, furnace or woodstove where the burn occurs; normally lined with firebrick or molded or sprayed insulation.

Compression web - A member of a truss system which connects the bottom and top chords, and which provides downward support.

Compressor - A mechanical device that pressurizes a gas in order to turn it into a liquid, thereby allowing heat to be removed or added. A compressor is the main component of conventional heat pumps and air conditioners. In an air conditioning system, the compressor normally sits outside and has a large fan (to remove heat).

Concrete - The mixture of Portland cement, sand, gravel, and water. Used to make garage and basement floors, sidewalks, patios, foundation walls, etc. It is commonly reinforced with steel rods (rebar) or wire screening (mesh).

Concrete block - A hollow concrete 'brick' often 8" x 8" x 16" in size.

Concrete board - A panel made out of concrete and fiberglass usually used as a tile backing material.

Condensation - Beads or drops of water (and frequently frost in extremely cold weather) that accumulate on the inside of the exterior covering of a building. Use of louvers or attic ventilators will reduce moisture condensation in attics. A vapor barrier under the gypsum lath or dry wall on exposed walls will reduce condensation.

Condensing unit - The outdoor component of a cooling system. It includes a compressor and condensing coil designed to give off heat.

Conditions, Covenants, and Restrictions (CC and Rs) - The standards that define how a property may be used and the protections the developer makes for the benefit of all owners in a subdivision.

Construction Contract - A legal document which specifies the what, when, where, how, how-much and by whom in a construction project. A good construction contract will generally include:

Contractor - A company licensed to perform certain types of construction activities. In most states, the general contractor's license and some specialty contractor's licenses don't require of compliance with bonding, workmen's compensation and similar regulations. Some of the specialty contractor licenses involve extensive training, testing and/or insurance requirements. There are various types of contractors:

- The contractor's registration number.

- A statement of work quality such as 'Standard Practices of the Trades' or 'according to Manufacturers Specifications'.

- A set of Blueprints or Plans.

- A construction timetable including starting and completion dates.

- A set of Specifications.

- A Fixed Price for the work, or a Time and Materials formula.

- A Payment Schedule.

- Any Allowances.

- A clause which outlines how any disputes will be resolved.

- A written warranty.

Contractor - A company licensed to perform certain types of construction activities. In most regions, the general contractor's license and some specialty contractor's licenses don't require of compliance with bonding, workmen's compensation and similar regulations. Some of the specialty contractor licenses involve extensive training, testing and/or insurance requirements.

There are various types of contractors:

- General contractor - responsible for the execution, supervision and overall coordination of a project and may also perform some of the individual construction tasks. Most general contractors are not licensed to perform all specialty trades and must hire specialty contractors for such tasks, e.g. electrical, plumbing.

- Remodeling contractor - a general contractor who specializes in remodeling work.

- Specialty contractor - licensed to perform a specialty task e.g. electrical, side sewer, asbestos abatement.

- Subcontractor - a general or specialty contractor who works for another general contractor.

Damper - A metal "door" placed within the fireplace chimney. Normally closed when the fireplace is not in use.

Dampproofing - The black, tar like waterproofing material applied to the exterior of a foundation wall.

Daylight - The end of a pipe (the terminal end) that is not attached to anything.

Dead bolt - An exterior security lock installed on exterior entry doors that can be activated only with a key or thumb-turn. Unlike a latch, which has a beveled tongue, dead bolts have square ends.

Dead light - The fixed, non-operable window section of a window unit.

Deck, decked - To install the plywood or wafer board sheeting on the floor joists, rafters, or trusses.

Dedicated circuit - An electrical circuit that serves only one appliance (i.e., dishwasher) or a series of electric heaters or smoke detectors.

Default - Breach of a mortgage contract (not making the required payments).

De-humidistat - A control mechanism used to operate a mechanical ventilation system based upon the relative humidity in the home.

Delamination - Separation of the plies in a panel due to failure of the adhesive. Usually caused by excessive moisture.

Disconnect - A large (generally 20 Amp) electrical ON-OFF switch.

Discount rate - A mortgage interest rate that is lower than the current rate for a certain period of time, e.g. 2.00% below variable rate for 2 years.

Doorjamb, interior - The surrounding case into which and out of which a door closes and opens. It consists of two upright pieces, called side jambs, and a horizontal head jamb. These 3 jambs have the "door stop" installed on them.

Door operator - An automatic garage door opener.

Door stop - The wooden style that the door slab will rest upon when it's in a closed position.

Dormer - An opening in a sloping roof, the framing of which projects out to form a vertical wall suitable for windows or other openings.

Double glass - Window or door in which two panes of glass are used with a sealed air space between. Also known as Insulating Glass.

Double hung window - A window with two vertically sliding sashes, both of which can move up and down.

Down payment - The difference between the sales price and the mortgage amount. A down payment is usually paid at closing.

Downspout - A pipe, usually of metal, for carrying rainwater down from the roof's horizontal gutters.

Drain tile - A perforated, corrugated plastic pipe laid at the bottom of the foundation wall and used to drain excess water away from the foundation. It prevents ground water from seeping through the foundation wall. Sometimes called perimeter drain.

Draw - The amount of progress billings on a contract that is currently available to a contractor under a contract with a fixed payment schedule.

Drip - (a) A member of a cornice or other horizontal exterior finish course that has a projection beyond the other parts for throwing off water. (b) A groove in the underside of a sill or drip cap to cause water to drop off on the outer edge instead of drawing back and running down the face of the building.

Drip cap - A molding or metal flashing placed on the exterior topside of a door or window frame to cause water to drip beyond the outside of the frame.

Dry in - To install the black roofing felt (tar paper) on the roof.

Drywall (or Gypsum Wallboard (GWB), Sheet rock or Plasterboard) - Wall board or gypsum - A manufactured panel made out of gypsum plaster and encased in a thin cardboard. Usually 1/2" thick and 4' x 8' or 4' x 12' in size. The panels are nailed or screwed onto the framing and the joints are taped and covered with a 'joint compound'. 'Green board' type drywall has a greater resistance to moisture than regular (white) plasterboard and is used in bathrooms and other "wet areas".

Ducts - The heating system. Usually round or rectangular metal pipes installed for distributing warm (or cold) air from the furnace to rooms in the home. Also, a tunnel made of galvanized metal or rigid fiberglass, which carries air from the heater or ventilation opening to the rooms in a building.

Due-on-sale - A clause in a mortgage contract requiring the borrower to pay the entire outstanding balance upon sale or transfer of the property.

Dura board, dura rock - A panel made out of concrete and fiberglass usually used as a ceramic tile backing material. Commonly used on bathtub decks. Sometimes called Wonder board.

DWV (drain-waste-vent) - The section of a plumbing system that carries water and sewer gases out of a home.

Easement - A formal contract which allows a party to use another party's property for a specific purpose. e.g. A sewer easement might allow one party to run a sewer line through a neighbor's property.

Eaves - The horizontal exterior roof overhang.

Egress - A means of exiting the home. An egress window is required in every bedroom and basement. Normally a 4' X 4' window is the minimum size required

Elbow (ell) - A plumbing or electrical fitting that lets you change directions in runs of pipe or conduit.

Electric lateral - The trench or area in the yard where the electric service line (from a transformer or pedestal) is located, or the work of installing the electric service to a home.

Electric resistance coils - Metal wires that heat up when electric current passes through them and are used in baseboard heaters and electric water heaters.

Electrical entrance package - The entry point of the electrical power including: (1) the 'strike' or location where the overhead or underground electrical lines connect to the house, (2) The meter which measures how much power is used and (3) The 'panel' or 'circuit breaker box' (or 'fuse box') where the power can be shut off and where overload devices such as fuses or circuit breakers are located.

Electrical Rough - Work performed by the Electrical Contractor after the plumber and heating contractor are complete with their phase of work. Normally all electrical wires, and outlet, switch, and fixture boxes are installed (before insulation).

Electrical Trim - Work performed by the electrical contractor when the house is nearing completion. The electrician installs all plugs, switches, light fixtures, smoke detectors, appliance "pig tails", bath ventilation fans, wires the furnace, and "makes up" the electric house panel. The electrician does all work necessary to get the home ready for and to pass the municipal electrical final inspection.

Elevation sheet - The page on the blueprints that depicts the house or room as if a vertical plane were passed through the structure.

Equity - The "valuation" that you own in your home, i.e. the property value less the mortgage loan outstanding.

Escrow - The handling of funds or documents by a third party on behalf of the buyer and/or seller.

Estimate - The amount of labor, materials, and other costs that a contractor anticipates for a project as summarized in the contractor's bid proposal for the project.

Estimating - The process of calculating the cost of a project. This can be a formal and exact process or a quick and imprecise process.

Extras - Additional work requested of a contractor, not included in the original plan, which will be billed separately and will not alter the original contract amount but increase the cost of building the home.

FHA strap - Metal straps that are used to repair a bearing wall "cut-out", and to "tie together" wall corners, splices, and bearing headers. Also, they are used to hang stairs and landings to bearing headers.

Face nail - To install nails into the vertical face of a bearing header or beam.

Faced concrete - To finish the front and all vertical sides of a concrete porch, step(s), or patio. Normally the "face" is broom finished.

Facing brick - The brick used and exposed on the outside of a wall. Usually these have a finished texture.

Fascia - Horizontal boards attached to rafter/truss ends at the eaves and along gables. Roof drain gutters are attached to the fascia.

Felt - Tar paper. Installed under the roof shingles. Normally 15 lb. or 30 lb.

Female - Any part, such as a nut or fitting, into which another (male) part can be inserted. Internal threads are female.

Ferrule - Metal tubes used to keep roof gutters "open". Long nails (ferrule spikes) are driven through these tubes and hold the gutters in place along the fascia of the home.

Field measure - To take measurements (cabinets, countertops, stairs, shower doors, etc.) in the home itself instead of using the blueprints.

Finger joint - A manufacturing process of interlocking two shorter pieces of wood end to end to create a longer piece of dimensional lumber or molding. Often used in jambs and casings and are normally painted (instead of stained).

Fire block - Short horizontal members sometimes nailed between studs, usually about halfway up a wall. See also 'Fire stop'.

Fire brick - Brick made of refractory ceramic material which will resist high temperatures. Used in a fireplace and boiler.

Fireplace chase flashing pan - A large sheet of metal that is installed around and perpendicular to the fireplace flue pipe. Its purpose is to confine and limit the spread of fire and smoke to a small area.

Fire-resistive or Fire rated - Applies to materials that are not combustible in the temperatures of ordinary fires and will withstand such fires for at least 1 hour. Drywall used in the garage and party walls are to be fire rated, 5/8", Type X.

Fire retardant chemical - A chemical or preparation of chemicals used to reduce the flammability of a material or to retard the spread of flame.

Fire stop - A solid, tight closure of a concealed space, placed to prevent the spread of fire and smoke through such a space. In a frame wall, this will usually consist of 2 by 4 cross blocking between studs. Work performed to slow the spread of fire and smoke in the walls and ceiling (behind the drywall). Includes stuffing wire holes in the top and bottom plates with insulation and installing blocks of wood between the wall studs at the drop soffit line. This is integral to passing a Rough Frame inspection. See also 'Fire block'.

Fishplate (gusset) - A wood or plywood piece used to fasten the ends of two members together at a butt joint with nails or bolts. Sometimes used at the junction of opposite rafters near the ridge line. Sometimes called a gang nail plate.

Fish tape - A long strip of spring steel used for fishing cables and for pulling wires through conduit.

Fixed price contract - A contract with a set price for the work. See Time and Materials Contract.

Fixed rate - A loan where the initial payments are based on a certain interest rate for a stated period. The rate payable will not change during this period regardless of changes in the lender's standard variable rate.

Fixed Rate Mortgage - A mortgage with an interest rate that remains the same over the years.

Flagstone (flagging or flags) - Flat stones (1 to 4 inches thick) used for walks, steps, floors, and vertical veneer (in lieu of brick).

Flakeboard - A manufactured wood panel made out of 1" - 2" wood chips and glue. Often used as a substitute for plywood in the exterior wall and roof sheathing. Also called OSB or wafer board.

Flame retention burner - An oil burner, designed to hold the flame near the nozzle surface. Generally the most efficient type for residential use.

Flashing - Sheet metal or other material used in roof and wall construction to protect a building from water seepage.

Flat mold - Thin wood strips installed over the butt seam of cabinet skins.

Flat paint - An interior paint that contains a high proportion of pigment and dries to a flat or lusterless finish.

Flatwork - Common word for concrete floors, driveways, basements, and sidewalks.

Floating - The next-to-last stage in concrete work, when you smooth off the job and bring water to the surface by using a hand float or bull float.

Floating wall - A non-bearing wall built on a concrete floor. It is constructed so that the bottom two horizontal plates can compress or pull apart if the concrete floor moves up or down. Normally built on basements and garage slabs.

Fluorescent lighting - A fluorescent lamp is a gas-filled glass tube with a phosphor coating on the inside. Gas inside the tube is ionized by electricity which causes the phosphor coating to glow. Normally with two pins that extend from each end.

Flue - Large pipe through which fumes escape from a gas water heater, furnace, or fireplace. Normally these flue pipes are double walled, galvanized sheet metal pipe and sometimes referred to as a "B Vent". Fireplace flue pipes are normally triple walled. In addition, nothing combustible shall be within one inch from the flue pipe.

Flue collar - Round metal ring which fits around the heat flue pipe after the pipe passes out of the roof.

Flue damper - An automatic door located in the flue that closes it off when the burner turns off; purpose is to reduce heat loss up the flue from the still-warm furnace or boiler.

Flue lining - 2-foot lengths, fire clay or terra-cotta pipe (round or square) and usually made in all ordinary flue sizes. Used for the inner lining of chimneys with the brick or masonry work done around the outside. Flue linings in chimneys runs from one foot below the flue connection to the top of the chimney.

Fly rafters - End rafters of the gable overhang supported by roof sheathing and lookouts.

Footer, footing - Continuous 8" or 10" thick concrete pad installed before and supports the foundation wall or monocots.

Forced air heating - A common form of heating with natural gas, propane, oil or electricity as a fuel. Air is heated in the furnace and distributed through a set of metal ducts to various areas of the house.

Form - Temporary structure erected to contain concrete during placing and initial hardening.

Foundation - The supporting portion of a structure below the first-floor construction, or below grade, including the footings.

Foundation ties - Metal wires that hold the foundation wall panels and rebar in place during the concrete pour.

Foundation waterproofing - High-quality below-grade moisture protection. Used for below-grade exterior concrete and masonry wall damp-proofing to seal out moisture and prevent corrosion. Normally looks like black tar.

Frame Inspection - The act of inspecting the home's structural integrity and its compliance to local municipal codes.

Framer - The carpenter contractor that installs the lumber and erects the frame, flooring system, interior walls, backing, trusses, rafters, decking, installs all beams, stairs, soffits and all work related to the wood structure of the home. The framer builds the home according to the blueprints and must comply with local building codes and regulations.

Framing - Lumber used for the structural members of a building, such as studs, joists, and rafters.

Frieze - In house construction a horizontal member connecting the top of the siding with the soffit of the cornice.

Frost lid - Round metal lid that is installed on a water meter pit.

Frost line - The depth of frost penetration in soil and/or the depth at which the earth will freeze and swell. This depth varies in different parts of the country.

Furring strips - Strips of wood, often 1 X 2 and used to shim out and provide a level fastening surface for a wall or ceiling.

Fuse - A device often found in older homes designed to prevent overloads in electrical lines. This protects against fire. See also 'circuit breakers'

General Contractor - A contractor who enters into a contract with the owner of a project for the construction of the project and who takes full responsibility for its completion, although the contractor may enter into subcontracts with others for the performance of specific parts or phases of the project.

Hardware - All of the "metal" fittings that go into the home when it is near completion. For example, doorknobs, towel bars, handrail brackets, closet rods, house numbers, door closers, etc. The Interior Trim Carpenter installs the "hardware".

Hazard insurance - Protection against damage caused by fire, windstorms, or other common hazards. Many lenders require borrowers to carry it in an amount at least equal to the mortgage.

Heat Rough - Work performed by the Heating Contractor after the stairs and interior walls are built. This includes installing all duct work and flue pipes. Sometimes, the furnace and fireplaces are installed at this stage of construction.

Heat Trim - Work done by the Heating Contractor to get the home ready for the municipal Final Heat Inspection. This includes venting the hot water heater, installing all vent grills, registers, air conditioning services, turning on the furnace, installing thermostats, venting ranges and hoods, and all other heat related work.

H V A C - An abbreviation for Heat, Ventilation, and Air Conditioning

Insulation - Any material high in resistance to heat transmission that, when placed in the walls, ceiling, or floors of a structure, and will reduce the rate of heat flow.

Kilowatt (kw) - One thousand watts. A kilowatt hour is the base unit used in measuring electrical consumption. Also see watt.

Manufacturer's specifications - The written installation and/or maintenance instructions which are developed by the manufacturer of a product and which may have to be followed in order to maintain the product warrantee.

Masonry - Stone, brick, concrete, hollow-tile, concrete block, or other similar building units or materials. Normally bonded together with mortar to form a wall.

Millwork - Generally all building materials made of finished wood and manufactured in millwork plants. Includes all doors, window and door frames, blinds, mantels, panelwork, stairway components (balusters, rail, etc.), moldings, and interior trim. Does not include flooring, ceiling, or siding.

Nail inspection - An inspection made by a municipal building inspector after the drywall material is hung with nails and screws (and before taping).

Natural finish - A transparent finish which does not seriously alter the original colour or grain of the natural wood. Natural finishes are usually provided by sealers, oils, varnishes, water repellent preservatives, and other similar materials.

NEC (National Electrical Code) - A set of rules governing safe wiring methods. Local codes—which are backed by law—may differ from the NEC in some ways.

Neutral wire - Usually colour-coded white, this carries electricity from an outlet back to the service panel. Also see hot wire and ground.

Newel post - The large starting post to which the end of a stair guard railing or balustrade is fastened.

Nonbearing wall - A wall supporting no load other than its own weight.

Nosing - The projecting edge of a molding or drip or the front edge of a stair tread.

Notch - A crosswise groove at the end of a board.

Note - A formal document showing the existence of a debt and stating the terms of repayment.

Nozzle - The part of a heating system that sprays the fuel of fuel-air mixture into the combustion chamber.

O C - On Center - The measurement of spacing for studs, rafters, and joists in a building from the center of one member to the center of the next.

Oakum - Loose hemp or jute fiber that's impregnated with tar or pitch and used to caulk large seams or for packing plumbing pipe joints

Open hole inspection - When an engineer (or municipal inspector) inspects the open excavation and examines the earth to determine the type of foundation (caisson, footer, wall on ground, etc.) that should be installed in the hole.

Oriented Strand Board or OSB - A manufactured 4' X 8' wood panel made out of 1" - 2" wood chips and glue. Often used as a substitute for plywood.

Outrigger - An extension of a rafter beyond the wall line. Usually, a smaller member nailed to a larger rafter to form a cornice or roof overhang.

Outside corner - The point at which two walls form an external angle, one you usually can walk around.

Overhang - Outward projecting eave-soffit area of a roof; the part of the roof that hangs out or over the outside wall. See also Cornice.

Payment schedule - A pre-agreed upon schedule of payments to a contractor usually based upon the amount of work completed. Such a schedule may include a deposit prior to the start of work. There may also be a temporary 'retainer' (5%-10% of the total cost of the job) at the end of the contract for correcting any small items which have not been completed or repaired.

Penalty clause - A provision in a contract that provides for a reduction in the amount otherwise payable under a contract to a contractor as a penalty for failure to meet deadlines or for failure of the project to meet contract specifications.

Performance bond - An amount of money (usually 10% of the total price of a job) that a contractor must put on deposit with a governmental agency as an insurance policy that guarantees the contractors' proper and timely completion of a project or job.

Permit - A governmental municipal authorization to perform a building process as in:

- Zoning\Use permit - Authorization to use a property for a specific use e.g. a garage, a single-family residence etc.

- Demolition permit - Authorization to tear down and remove an existing structure.

- Grading permit - Authorization to change the contour of the land.

- Septic permit - A health department authorization to build or modify a septic system.

- Building permit - Authorization to build or modify a structure.

- Electrical permit - A separate permit required for most electrical work.

- Plumbing permit - A separate permit required for new plumbing and larger modifications of existing plumbing systems.

Plumbing rough - Work performed by the plumbing contractor after the Rough Heat is installed. This work includes installing all plastic ABS drain and waste lines, copper water lines, bathtubs, shower pans, and gas piping to furnaces and fireplaces. Lead solder should not be used on copper piping.

Plumbing trim - Work performed by the plumbing contractor to get the home ready for a final plumbing inspection. Includes installing all toilets (water closets), hot water heaters, sinks, connecting all gas pipe to appliances, disposal, dishwasher, and all plumbing items.

Punch list - A list of discrepancies that need to be corrected by the contractor.

Radiant heating - A method of heating, usually consisting of a forced hot water system with pipes placed in the floor, wall, or ceiling. Also electrically heated panels.

Radiation - Energy transmitted from a heat source to the air around it. Radiators actually depend more on convection than radiation.

Radon - A naturally occurring, heavier than air, radioactive gas common in many parts of the country. Radon gas exposure is associated with lung cancer. Mitigation measures may involve crawl space and basement venting and various forms of vapor barriers.

Radon system - A ventilation system beneath the floor of a basement and/or structural wood floor and designed to fan exhaust radon gas to the outside of the home.

Rafter - Lumber used to support the roof sheeting and roof loads. Generally, 2 X 10's and 2 X 12's are used. The rafters of a flat roof are sometimes called roof joists.

Rafter, hip - A rafter that forms the intersection of an external roof angle.

Rafter, valley - A rafter that forms the intersection of an internal roof angle. The valley rafter is normally made of double 2-inch-thick members.

Rail - Cross members of panel doors or of a sash. Also, a wall or open balustrade placed at the edge of a staircase, walkway bridge, or elevated surface to prevent people from falling off. Any relatively lightweight horizontal element, especially those found in fences (split rail).

Railroad tie - Black, tar and preservative impregnated, 6" X 8" and 6'-8' long wooden timber that was used to hold railroad track in place. Normally used as a member of a retaining wall.

Rake - Slope or slanted.

Rake fascia - The vertical face of the sloping end of a roof eave.

Rake siding - The practice of installing lap siding diagonally

Ranch - A single story, one level home.

Ready mixed concrete - Concrete mixed at a plant or in trucks en route to a job and delivered ready for placement.

Rebar, reinforcing bar - Ribbed steel bars installed in foundation concrete walls, footers, and poured in place concrete structures designed to strengthen concrete. Comes in various thickness' and strength grade.

Receptacle - An electrical outlet. A typical household will have many 120-volt receptacles for plugging in lams and appliances and 240-volt receptacles for the range, clothes dryer, air conditioners, etc.

Recording fee - A charge for recording the transfer of a property, paid to a city, county, or other appropriate branch of government.

Redline, red lined prints - Blueprints that reflect changes and that are marked with red pencil.

Reducer - A fitting with different size openings at either end and used to go from a larger to a smaller pipe.

Reflective insulation - Sheet material with one or both faces covered with aluminum foil.

Refrigerant - A substance that remains a gas at low temperatures and pressure and can be used to transfer heat. Freon is an example and is used in air conditioning systems.

Register - A grill placed over a heating duct or cold air return.

Reglaze - To replace a broken window.

Relief valve - A device designed to open if it detects excess temperature or pressure.

Remote - Remote electrical, gas, or water meter digital readouts that are installed near the front of the home in order for utility companies to easily read the homeowners usage of the service.

Retaining wall - A structure that holds back a slope and prevents erosion.

Retentions - Amounts withheld from progress billings until final and satisfactory project completion.

R factor or value - A measure of a materials resistance to the passage of heat. New home walls are usually insulated with 4" of batt insulation with an R value of R-24, and a ceiling insulation of R-60.

Ribbon (girt) - Normally a 1 X 4 board let into the studs horizontally to support the ceiling or second-floor joists.

Ridge - The horizontal line at the junction of the top edges of two sloping roof surfaces.

Ridge board - The board placed on the ridge of the roof onto which the upper ends of other rafters are fastened.

Ridge shingles - Shingles used to cover the ridge board.

Rim joist - A joist that runs around the perimeter of the floor joists and home.

Rise - The vertical distance from the eaves line to the ridge. Also, the vertical distance from stair tread to stair tread (and not to exceed 7 ½").

Riser - Each of the vertical boards closing the spaces between the treads of stairways.

Riser and panel - The exterior vertical pipe (riser) and metal electric box (panel) the electrician provides and installs at the "Rough Electric" stage.

Road base - A aggregate mixture of sand and stone.

Rock 1, 2, 3 - When referring to drywall, this means to install drywall to the walls and ceilings (with nails and screws), and before taping is performed.

Roll, rolling - To install the floor joists or trusses in their correct place. (To "roll the floor" means to install the floor joists).

Roll roofing - Asphalt roofing products manufactured in roll form. 36-inch -wide rolls with and 108 square feet of material. Weights are generally 45 to 90 pounds per roll.

Romex - A name brand of nonmetallic sheathed electrical cable that is used for indoor wiring.

Roof jack - Sleeves that fit around the black plumbing waste vent pipes at, and are nailed to, the roof sheeting.

Roof joist - The rafters of a flat roof. Lumber used to support the roof sheeting and roof loads. Generally, 2 X 10's and 2 X 12's are used.

Roof sheathing or sheeting - The wood panels or sheet material fastened to the roof rafters or trusses on which the shingle or other roof covering is laid.

Roof valley - The "V" created where two sloping roofs meet.

Rough opening - The horizontal and vertical measurement of a window or door opening before drywall or siding is installed.

Rough sill - The framing member at the bottom of a rough opening for a window. It is attached to the cripple studs below the rough opening.

Roughing-in - The initial stage of a plumbing, electrical, heating, carpentry, and/or other project, when all components that won't be seen after the second finishing phase are assembled. See also Heat Rough, Plumbing Rough, and Electrical Rough.

Run, roof - The horizontal distance from the eaves to a point directly under the ridge. One half the span.

Run, stair - the horizontal distance of a stair tread from the nose to the riser.

R Value - A measure of insulation. A measure of a materials resistance to the passage of heat. The higher the R value, the more insulating "power" it has. For example, typical new home's walls are usually insulated with 4" of batt insulation with an R value of R-13, and a ceiling insulation of R-30.

Saddle - A small second roof built behind the back side of a fireplace chimney to divert water around the chimney. Also, the plate at the bottom of some—usually exterior—door openings. Sometimes called a threshold.

Sack mix - The amount of Portland cement in a cubic yard of concrete mix. Generally, 5 or 6 sack is required in a foundation wall.

Sales contract - A contract between a buyer and seller which should explain: (1) What the purchase includes, (2) What guarantees there are, (3) When the buyer can move in, (4) What the closing costs are, and (5) What recourse the parties have if the contract is not fulfilled or if the buyer cannot get a mortgage commitment at the agreed upon time.

Sand float finish - Lime that is mixed with sand, resulting in a textured finish on a wall.

Sanitary sewer - A sewer system designed for the collection of wastewater from the bathroom, kitchen and laundry drains, and is usually not designed to handle storm water.

Sash - A single light frame containing one or more lights of glass. The frame that holds the glass in a window, often the movable part of the window.

Sash balance - A device, usually operated by a spring and designed to hold a single hung window vent up and in place.

Saturated felt - A felt which is impregnated with tar or asphalt.

Schedule (window, door, mirror) - A table on the blueprints that list the sizes, quantities and locations of the windows, doors and mirrors.

Scrap out - The removal of all drywall material and debris after the home is "hung out" (installed) with drywall.

Scratch coat - The first coat of plaster, which is scratched to form a bond for a second coat.

Screed, concrete - To level off concrete to the correct elevation during a concrete pour.

Screed, plaster - A small strip of wood, usually the thickness of the plaster coat, used as a guide for plastering.

Scribing - Cutting and fitting woodwork to an irregular surface.

Scupper - (1) An opening for drainage in a wall, curb or parapet. (2) The drain in a downspout or flat roof, usually connected to the downspout.

Sealer - A finishing material, either clear or pigmented, that is usually applied directly over raw wood for the purpose of sealing the wood surface.

Seasoning - Drying and removing moisture from green wood in order to improve its usability.

Self-sealing shingles - Shingles containing factory-applied strips or spots of self-sealing adhesive.

Semigloss paint or enamel - A paint or enamel made so that its coating, when dry, has some luster but is not very glossy. Bathrooms and kitchens are normally painted semi-gloss.

Septic system - An onsite wastewater treatment system. It usually has a septic tank which promotes the biological digestion of the waste, and a drain field which is designed to let the left-over liquid soak into the ground. Septic systems and permits are usually sized by the number of bedrooms in a house.

Service entrance panel - Main power cabinet where electricity enters a home wiring system.

Service equipment - Main control gear at the service entrance, such as circuit breakers, switches, and fuses.

Service lateral - Underground power supply line.

Setback Thermostat - A thermostat with a clock which can be programmed to come on or go off at various temperatures and at different times of the day/week. Usually used as the heating or cooling system thermostat.

Settlement - Shifts in a structure, usually caused by freeze-thaw cycles underground.

Sewage ejector - A pump used to 'lift' wastewater to a gravity sanitary sewer line. Usually used in basements and other locations which are situated below the level of the side sewer.

Sewer lateral - The portion of the sanitary sewer which connects the interior wastewater lines to the main sewer lines. The side sewer is usually buried in several feet of soil and runs from the house to the sewer line. It is usually 'owned' by the sewer utility, must be maintained by the owner and may only be serviced by utility approved contractors. Sometimes called side sewer.

Sewer stub - The junction at the municipal sewer system where the home's sewer line is connected.

Sewer tap - The physical connection point where the home's sewer line connects to the main municipal sewer line.

Shake - A wood roofing material, normally cedar or redwood. Produced by splitting a block of the wood along the grain line. Modern shakes are sometimes machine sawn on one side. See shingle.

Shear block - Plywood that is face nailed to short (2 X 4's or 2 X 6's) wall studs (above a door or window, for example). This is done to prevent the wall from sliding and collapsing.

Sheathing, sheeting - The structural wood panel covering, usually OSB or plywood, used over studs, floor joists or rafters/trusses of a structure.

Shed roof - A roof containing only one sloping plane.

Sheet metal work - All components of a house employing sheet metal, such as flashing, gutters, and downspouts.

Specifications or Specs - A narrative list of materials, methods, model numbers, colours, allowances, and other details which supplement the information contained in the blueprints. Written elaboration in specific detail about construction materials and methods. Written to supplement working drawings.

Standard practices of the trade(s) - One of the more common basic and minimum construction standards. In other words, the work should be done in the way it is normally done by the average professional in the field.

Take off - The material necessary to complete a job.

Time and materials contract - A construction contract which specifies a price for different elements of the work such as cost per hour of labour, overhead, profit, etc. A contract which may not have a maximum price, or may state a 'price not to exceed'.

Trim (plumbing, heating, electrical) - The work that the "mechanical" contractors perform to finish their respective aspects of work, and when the home is nearing completion and occupancy.

Trim - Interior - The finish materials in a building, such as moldings applied around openings (window trim, door trim) or at the floor and ceiling of rooms (baseboard, cornice, and other moldings). Also, the physical work of installing interior doors and interior woodwork, to include all handrails, guardrails, stair way balustrades, mantles, light boxes, base, door casings, cabinets, countertops, shelves, windowsills and aprons, etc. Exterior - The finish materials on the exterior a building, such as moldings applied around openings (window trim, door trim), siding, windows, exterior doors, attic vents, crawl space vents, shutters, etc. Also, the physical work of installing these materials.

Turnkey - A term used when the subcontractor provides all materials (and labour) for a job.

Voltage - A measure of electrical potential. Most homes are wired with 110 - and 220-volt lines. The 110-volt power is used for lighting and most of the other circuits. The 220-volt power is usually used for the kitchen range, hot water heater and dryer

Walk-Through - A final inspection of a home before "Closing" to look for and document problems that need to be corrected.

Warranty - In construction there are two general types of warranties. One is provided by the manufacturer of a product such as roofing material or an appliance. The second is a warranty for the labour. For example, a roofing contract may include a 20-year material warranty and a 5-year labour warranty. Many new homebuilders provide a new-home warranty. Any major issue found during the first year should be communicated to the builder immediately. Small items can be saved up and presented to the builder for correction periodically through the first year after closing.

Weatherization - Work on a building exterior in order to reduce energy consumption for heating or cooling. Work involving adding insulation, installing storm windows and doors, caulking cracks and putting on weather-stripping.

Zone - The section of a building that is served by one heating or cooling loop because it has noticeably distinct heating or cooling needs. Also, the section of property that will be watered from a lawn sprinkler system.

Zoning - A governmental process and specification which limits the use of a property e.g. single-family use, high rise residential use, industrial use, etc. Zoning laws may limit where you can locate a structure. Also see building codes.

For more information about Premier Quality Renovations contact:

Peter Glaw

info@premier-renovations.com

www.premier-renovations.com

1-905-286-0303

To become a part of our mailing list

for the latest news in renovations and remodeling,

go to www.premierpress.ca

Book an Onsite or Virtual Consultation Now

Call: 1-905-286-0303
Email: info@premier-renovations.com
www.premier-renovations.com/contact-us

Start Saving Thousands of Dollars
on your reno no matter who does your renovation...

Go To
www.premier-renovations.com/access

Request Your Access Card Now